Panther Chameleons

The Complete Guide to Owning this Amazing Pet Lizard

By Richard G. Shaw

Disclaimer and legal notice

- The information in this book is provided and sold with the knowledge that the publisher and author do not offer any legal, medical or other professional advice. In the case of a need for any such expertise consult with the appropriate professional. This book does not contain all information available on the subject. This book has not been created to be specific to any individual's or organizations' situation or needs.

- Although the author and publisher have made every effort to ensure that the information in this book was correct at press time, the author and publisher do not assume and hereby disclaim any liability to any party for any loss, damage, or disruption caused by errors or omissions, whether such errors or omissions result from negligence, accident, or any other cause.

- This book is not intended as a substitute for the medical advice of physicians. The reader should regularly consult a physician in matters relating to health and particularly with respect to any symptoms that may require diagnosis or medical attention.

- In the interest of full disclosure, this book may contain affiliate links that might pay the author or publisher a commission upon any purchase from the company. While the author and publisher take no responsibility for the business practices of these companies and or the performance of any product or service, the author or publisher has used any such product or service and makes a recommendation in good faith based on that experience.

Table of Contents

Chapter 1: Introduction

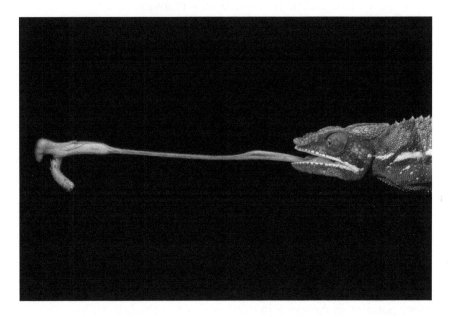

The days when having a pet meant owning a dog, cat, rabbit, fish, or hamster are long gone. The range of pets found in homes today has broadened to include *exotic pets* such as chameleons.

Whether one defines an exotic pet as one that isn't a standard or usual pet or as from a species that comes from a location other than one's own, the panther chameleon fits the definition.

Here are some astonishing chameleon facts to whet your appetite:

- ✓ **Just under half of the world's chameleon species come from the island of Madagascar**.

- ✓ **Chameleon's eyes have a 360-degree arc of vision and can see two directions at once,** giving them stereoscopic vision and incredibly accurate depth perception.

- ✓ They can spot prey, including small insects, from sixteen to thirty-two feet or five to ten meters away.

- ✓ Chameleons can see in both visible and ultraviolet light.

- ✓ Chameleons don't have an outer or a middle ear, so there is no ear opening or eardrum.

- ✓ A chameleon can change color in as little as 20 seconds.

- ✓ It takes 0.07 seconds to unroll their tongue which is then shot out to a distance that is one and a half or twice the length of the chameleon's body.

The panther chameleon is the most beautiful chameleon of the species and also one of the largest. These chameleons have been imported into various countries for several decades and have been very popular in America in particular since the late 1970s.

Their natural habitat is the tropical forests in the northern and eastern parts of the island country of Madagascar that lies in the Indian Ocean and off the south-east coast of Africa. They are also found on the islands of Mauritius and Reunion.

What makes the panther chameleon both striking and desirable as a pet is, firstly, its size and, secondly, the range of spectacular colors that they are found in. These colors include blue, red, green, pink, tan, peach, and orange. Patterns and colors vary depending on the area the chameleon comes from.

This book aims to introduce you to these remarkable members of the lizard family by describing their temperament, behavior, needs, and biology. It will also tell you what you need to know in order to decide whether or not this is the pet for you and, if it is, where to buy one, how to select your panther chameleon, what you need to buy, and how to take proper care of your fantastic new pet.

Please note that some of the information in this book is not specific to the panther chameleon but can be applied to all chameleon species. I hope that you find this book both useful and fun to read!

Chapter 2: What Makes Them Amazing Pets?

There are a number of reasons why panther chameleons are really great and amazing pets. These will not only convince you, if you are still undecided, but can also be presented to a parent, spouse, or partner who is not keen on you getting one!

Here are some of the main reasons why a panther chameleon is *the* pet for you:

❖ They are the most striking of all chameleon species; they are gorgeous to look at.

❖ Despite the fact that they move slowly, they are such unique creatures that they are fascinating to watch.

❖ They are amazing to learn about, and owning one teaches you about ecology, eco systems, reptiles, the panther chameleon specifically, chameleons in general, and life skills like planning, organizing, and responsibility.

❖ They have definite personalities that emerge as the chameleon matures.

❖ Because they are a popular lizard pet you shouldn't have a problem finding a vet that knows how to handle and treat them.

❖ They don't smell at all. Even their fecal matter doesn't smell… unless the chameleon is unwell.

❖ They don't make any noise except the odd rustle as they move about in the leaves.

❖ They move slowly so they are unlikely to escape.

❖ They don't leave hair all over your furniture and clothes.

❖ They don't need to be taken for walks.

Chapter 3: Is it the Right Pet for You?

1) Questions to ask yourself before you buy a panther chameleon

So, you've decided you want an exotic rather than a traditional pet. In addition, you have opted to get a reptile rather than, for instance, an unusual mammal like a potbellied pig or a hedgehog.

However, before you head off to buy your panther chameleon you need to ask yourself some questions and answer them truthfully… for your sake and the sake of your new pet!

➢ Can you afford to own one of these lizards? Depending on its age and where it is from, a panther chameleon will set you back between $140 and $600. And that is just the start!

There are also the other various once-off and start-up costs such as the enclosure; furnishings such as plants and so on; and lighting, heating, cleaning, and the misting equipment. These will be discussed in detail in a later chapter.

➢ Do you have the necessary space in your home? Reptiles of various kinds need an enclosure that is big enough for them to live in happily when they are fully grown. Chameleons require enough space to house the environment that they need or they become stressed and / or sick.

➢ Are you up to the challenge of housing live food and giving it to your chameleon? Using dried crickets, for example, is not an option. Whatever prey you will be feeding your lizard pet must be live. Not all pet owners can cope with this aspect.

➢ Do you have the financial resources to handle the regular or monthly expenses? These will include food, increased utilities bills, enclosure equipment, cleaning materials, and vet bills when your chameleon is not well. Again, these costs will be discussed further at a later stage.

2) The advantages of these pet lizards

There are a number of advantages when it comes to anther chameleons as pets in addition to their stunning colors! The main ones include:

✓ They are fascinating to watch, learn about, and to care for.

✓ They have no odor. If your chameleon smells there is something seriously wrong! Even their feces and urine, which is combined, does not smell bad.

7

✓ They are really quiet… unless the slight rustling of leaves when they move around on a branch or vine is going to bother you.

✓ They move very slowly so even if your chameleon escapes it certainly won't be a quick getaway, and you will be able to get him or her back.

✓ Their live food, if you get the right kind, also doesn't smell or make a noise.

✓ Having a panther chameleon teaches you a great deal about habitats and the environment.

✓ Because they need regular maintenance, they can teach you planning and scheduling skills.

The last two in particular will help you convince your parents or partner or spouse that these are excellent pets to have!

3) The disadvantages of having a chameleon

As with many things there is, inevitably, a downside. Before buying a panther chameleon you need to know what they are and decide if you can deal with them or not. If you have any doubts you should not get a panther chameleon or perhaps any kind of chameleon or even a reptile.

The primary disadvantages are:

▪ They are not easy to care for because their environment has to be exactly right at all times

▪ Their food must be clean and free of bacteria and parasites.

- The care requirements mean that a chameleon is *not* the pet for a beginner!

- Panther chameleons are expensive and the equipment you will need does not come cheap either. There are ongoing costs such as food, equipment, and potential vet bills. Many of these expenses apply not only to caring for and feeding the chameleon but also its food!

- You need to have a regular care and maintenance schedule. If you can't meet it, then you need someone who is willing to do so in your absence. Making sure that a chameleon has food, water, and that the necessary conditions are maintained can be a lot to ask from someone else.

- They are not "cuddly" pets and don't enjoy being handled. In fact, they are prone to become stressed if they are handled too much.

- Although with the correct hygiene practices it can be avoided, there is the risk of contracting Salmonella from reptiles.

- The care and health considerations make reptiles an unsuitable pet for a child younger than five years old and even for older children unless a parent is prepared to do a great deal of helping.

- While they are beautiful and interesting to watch, the fascination can wear off after a while if you are someone who gets bored by routines (maintenance) and wants a pet with a wide range of behaviors.

4) Panther chameleons versus other reptile pets

Which reptile you should get will be a highly personal choice, but there are some general guidelines that may help you make this decision.

Snakes:

Most snakes don't like being handled although some tolerate it fairly well. They can be very good at hiding and doing nothing, which means they are not usually an exciting pet to have or to watch. Children, in particular, can get bored with a snake quite quickly.

They also need the right conditions or environment in order to stay healthy. Some have to be fed live prey, such as mice, which is a major turn-off for many people. Finally, many snakes are excellent escape artists.

Bearded dragons:

These are very popular lizards and can be a good bet for a first-time pet owner or a young owner. They are said to have great personalities and are described as placid. They get used to being handled, and many owners say they are able to interact with these lizards. They are lively reptiles and therefore fun to watch.

However, young bearded dragons have to be fed three times a day, and this species requires a very hot cage. Also, adults can grow up to two feet or 0.6 meters in length.

Iguanas:

These large lizards are hard to care for. They are not considered suitable for children or first-time reptile owners. Their sheer size makes them difficult, even potentially dangerous, to handle. This is especially true for children or the inexperienced reptile or pet owner.

They are also vegetarians and therefore need a diet that is varied. This means buying, washing, chopping, and shredding a great deal of plant material every day. Children can't do this, and parents may not want to!

Monitor lizards:

These are also large, sometimes very large, lizards that are carnivorous or omnivorous. They need live prey as food and the right kind of environment.

They can be difficult, even dangerous, to handle because of their size and, on occasion, their temperaments. Some monitor lizards have been known to be fairly aggressive, and they have quite sharp claws.

Frogs and salamanders:

Little amphibians like frogs and Salamanders should be handled as little as possible. They can be easily stressed, and are only a good bet if you just want to look at a pet and maintain its environment.

They are especially not a good option for children as rough handling can easily cause injury, even death.

The Berber or Schneider skink and the blue-tongue skink:

The blue-tongue skink grows to up to 30 inches or 76 centimeters in length and requires a really big terrarium. They are omnivorous and need a diet of insects and vegetables. They can become quite tame. On the down side, they can be expensive to buy.

The Berber or Schneider skink is smaller: 18 inches or 46 centimeters. They prefer insects, but do also eat plants and should be given some plant material a couple of times a week.

So, to summarize…

Choose a reptile pet with these guidelines in mind:

- No pet is 100% easy to care for; some are just easier than others.

- Reptiles that spend of lot of time sleeping or hidden may well become neglected when an owner becomes bored with them or tired of the work that goes with caring for them.

- Don't buy a cute baby reptile without finding out how big it will be as an adult; you may not have space for it.

- Don't buy a reptile that is so rare or relatively unknown that you won't find a vet that knows how to care for one.

The panther chameleon scores well with all of these with the exception of the first item as they do require a lot of care. These chameleons are great to watch, do not grow too large, and can be treated by most vets!

Chapter 4: Its Origins

1) The place of origin of the panther chameleon

The panther chameleon is a reptile belonging to the zoological family Chamaeleonidea and its genus or scientific name is *Furcifer Pardalis*. Chameleons are highly specialized lizards.

These amazing creatures are found in coastal regions and in the low-lying sections of the lush, humid tropical forests in the northern, central, and eastern parts of Madagascar, an island that lies in the Indian Ocean off the south-east coast of Africa. Populations of panther chameleons have also been introduced into the nearby islands of Mauritius and Reunion.

Panther chameleons come in different colors and patterns depending on where or which specific area they come from. Although it is virtually impossible to know what area females are from, males from various locales are distinctive because of their colors.

When you buy a chameleon from a reputable dealer or breeder the name before the word "panther" will indicate which area it comes from. For example, the beautiful emerald-green, blue-green, or turquoise males from the Madagascan island of Nosy Be will be called, *Nosy Be panther chameleons*. Panther chameleons come from the islands around Madagascar in addition to the main island. Some of these islands are Nosy Be, Nosy Mitsio, Tamatave, Diego Suarez, Andapa, and Sambava.

Each area and island produces chameleons with distinctive patterns and colors. These include spots and stripes, and the spectrum of colors runs from pinks or yellowish-white, through the greens and blues, to reds and oranges. Each color will also vary in intensity. Generally colors become darker during the mating season or if the chameleon is aggressive in the presence of a rival or threat.

As with many species the females are less striking and are often found in brown, pale green, or grey. This changes, though, during breeding. Females who are ready to mate often become either a pale or a vibrant pink or orange. When they are gravid, or carrying eggs, they usually turn black with bars or stripes down their sides in bright pink or orange.

2) The history of the panther chameleon as a pet

Panther chameleons are probably the most well known, and certainly one of the most popular, of the pet chameleons. As indicated previously the main reasons for this are how beautiful they are, that they are a little less difficult to care for than other types, and because they can be taught to be more interactive.

It is not known when these lizards initially arrived on the pet market and first became popular with reptile owners. However, the export figures that are available on *arkive.org* indicate that the panther chameleon constituted approximately 8% of all the chameleons imported into America during the years 1977 to 2001.

This rising popularity, and the resultant increase in the number of wild chameleons being captured for the exotic pet market, began to cause concern, and trade quotas were implemented to protect these lizards. Fortunately, although they are found in a limited number of areas, panther chameleons are abundant in the wild.

3) Myths & misunderstandings about chameleons

They change color to camouflage themselves

This is probably the most common and persistent myth about all chameleons. It is now believed that the color changes chameleons undergo have very little to do with blending in or camouflage and more to do with internal reasons rather than the environment.

Although the camouflage theory has been disproved by scientists there is still some disagreement, or at least uncertainty, about why chameleons change their color and patterns. The main theories are:

15

- A color change is a visual signal that tells other chameleons about their mood (anger, stress, sexually receptive, and so forth).

- It indicates temperature or a change in temperature in either the chameleon or its environment.

- It is a way to communicate with other chameleons. For instance, lighter colored and/or multicolored males are often courting females, and dark females are often gravid (carrying eggs) and therefore not receptive to courting.

All of these seem possible or even likely, and further studies of these fascinating lizards should confirm one or more of these theories... or give rise to new ones!

They are endangered

This is untrue at the time of writing. According to the IUCN red list it was classified as "least concern," which means it is not endangered
Prior to 1999, about 15,000 chameleons were captured and exported annually, mainly to the US. This was an alarming figure and a maximum export quota was implemented in order to protect the species.

This quota is strictly controlled and regulated in order to protect the chameleons. Of course there is a black market for many creatures, and the panther chameleon is no exception. By only buying these lizards from a reputable dealer, you can be sure that you are not contributing to the black market demand.

The other threat that these chameleons face is the loss of their natural habitat. Fortunately, this is not too marked at present and the panther chameleon seems to be resistant in terms of this environmental threat.

These sought-after reptiles are currently found in abundance in the wild and are also fairly easy to breed in captivity. Both of these factors mean that at this point they are not endangered.

Owning them is illegal

This is only partially or marginally true. The panther chameleon is not illegal in the vast majority of countries, states, and counties. However, there are the odd exceptions.

For instance, although there is some confusion on the point, it appears that residents of the American state of Maine require a permit in order to own a panther chameleon, but ownership is not illegal.

Hawaii and Australia, on the other hand, have placed a complete ban on all non-indigenous or non-endemic chameleon species. These countries enforce this ban strictly in order to protect species that are endemic to their regions.

Chapter 5: General Information

1) The biology of these amazing lizards

The panther chameleon is a fairly large chameleon. Although those kept in captivity may be smaller, the average length for a male is 20 inches or 50 centimeters. Females are smaller, and they grow to 14 inches or 35 centimeters. Adult males weigh in at between 200 and 220 grams (7 to 7.5 ounces), and the female's weight range is 140 to 160 grams (5 to 5.6 ounces).

Chameleons generally have several physical features that stand out and are unique to them:

Eyes:

The chameleon's eyes are a most striking feature. The eyes, which are located on either side of the head, are dome-shaped and can rotate independently. The eyelids are fused, and there is only a pinhole-like opening for the pupil.

Because they move independently, each eye can look at and focus on a different area or thing. In addition, the ability to rotate their eyes in this way allows these extraordinary lizards to have a panoramic view of the environment. This allows them to hunt for prey and look out for predators or any other potential threats.

Tongue:

The tongue of the chameleon is also amazing, and it is designed for one thing: capturing prey. For decades it was thought that the tip of the tongue was sticky and that's how the insect was caught. However, it has been established that it is far more complex than that--the tongue also contains a suction device thanks to its extraordinary structure.

This is due to the fact that the tongue is actually an incredibly complex organ consisting of muscles, cartilage, glands, and nerves. The tongue is shot out at great speed, and to a distance of two and a half times the length of the chameleon's body, thanks to this mechanism.

Hunting and how prey is caught is discussed in more detail later in this chapter.

Feet:

The feet are also specialized and allow these lizards to grip onto branches, vines, etc. A chameleon's feet look almost like mittens or tongs because a foot has five toes, but they are fused into a group of two and a group of three. On the front feet, the group of three is on the inside of the foot. On the back feet, the group of three is on the outside.

19

This arrangement of fused toes gives the chameleon the ability to grasp a range of structures that lie either vertically or horizontally. Their very strong grip is further increased thanks to the presence of small but very sharp claws on each toe.

Tail:

The panther chameleon has a prehensile tail which performs several functions. First, it helps with climbing through vegetation as the tail can be used to grip branches. Secondly, the tail also helps the reptile to keep its balance as it navigates through foliage. Finally, it is rolled up when a chameleon is adopting a threatening or defensive posture as the rolled tail makes it look larger than it actually is.

Ears and nose:

In terms of the other senses, chameleons lack an outer and middle ear which means that, in all probability, they are deaf.

In addition, these lizards don't have a vomeronasal organ, which means they are unlikely to be able to smell anything.

2) How they catch their prey

The panther chameleon, like all chameleons, moves slowly which means they don't stalk prey as many other creatures do. They wait until food comes within reach of their astonishing tongues.

If they can be said to hunt, it is by looking for prey as they move through the vegetation. As soon as one of the chameleon's eyes sees prey, the head turns in that direction so that both eyes can focus on the meal-to-be. This allows the chameleon to very accurately determine distance to the prey.

The tongue, which stays coiled in the mouth when it is not in use, is then uncoiled and shot out of the mouth. The speed with which this happens is truly remarkable: the tongue uncoils in under 0.07 seconds, and the tongue shoots out at a staggering 1640 feet or 500 meters per second!

This phenomenal speed and movement is thanks to a combination of contracting the circular muscles in the tongue and relaxing the longitudinal muscles in the tongue which causes the lightning-quick uncurling and stretching of the organ.

The end of the tongue hits the prey, ideally on its head, and thanks to the stickiness and the suction created by the hollow at the tongue-tip, the prey is caught and held.

The muscle movements then reverse as the circular muscles relax and the longitudinal ones in the chameleon's tongue contract. The tongue returns to the mouth at speed and the insect is drawn into the mouth and then ground up between the chameleon's jaws.

3) How chameleons change color

While the *why* of changing color is fairly easy to discuss, the *how* is more complex and technical. Essentially the process is a molecular one.

The surface layer of the chameleon's skin is transparent. Below this layer are several separate layers of highly specialized cells called chromatophores. These cells all contain pigments or colors.

Each layer of chromatophores contains a different pigment or color. For instance, xanthophores contain yellow, erythrophores contain a red color, iridiphores contain a blue pigment called guanine, and finally melanophores, which contain a brown pigment called melanin. The colors are contained within the cells in tiny sacs called vesicles. This containment means that the colors don't color the cells all the time.

The various layers of chromatophores are affected by chemicals in the chameleon's blood and signals from its nervous system. When a chromatophore picks up a signal, such as anger or fear, the vesicles within a cell release the pigment or color, and it fills the cell with color.

When several layers of different chromatophores or colors change at the same time, and to varying degrees, the effect is rather like mixing paints: the range of possible colors and patterns are endless and lovely to see.

4) Life span

The lifespan for the panther chameleon in the wild is estimated to be between one and three years. This is largely due to predation and /or loss of habitat. The average life expectancy for a male chameleon in captivity is five years, although some have been known to live for as long as eight years.

Females lay eggs and live approximately half the time of their male counterparts. This is because egg-laying takes a heavy toll on their systems.

5) General considerations

Getting one or two Chameleons

It is important to note that chameleons are both solitary and territorial by nature. This basic nature is not affected either by the age or sex of the chameleon. As with most animals there are personality differences from one individual to the next.

However, their basic nature means that you should not put sub-adult or adult chameleons in a cage together. Each one should be housed separately. But that doesn't mean you can only have one panther chameleon!

Buying a male or a female

When it comes to selecting a male or female chameleon there are a number of factors to consider including:

- Females are not territorial so they are usually, but not always, less aggressive than the males. One can encounter females that are aggressive and, like some males, may even bite. (A chameleon bite is not serious, but it is painful as it feels like a hard pinch.)

- Males might be better for a first-time owner because he or she won't have to contend with eggs being laid and all the extra knowledge and work that goes with that. Having a male is often a good learning experience and practice run for getting a female.

- While females are not drab or colorless by any means, the male panther chameleons are far more colorful. If looks are important to you, then a male would be a better choice. One should keep in mind, though, that the full glorious colors won't appear until the chameleon is six to seven months old. Making sure a baby chameleon is correctly sexed is therefore important from this point of view.

- Males can grow to roughly twice the size of females. If you have limited space for your chameleon's cage, then a female would be better.

Keeping chameleons together or apart

The idea of keeping several of the same species of chameleon in the same cage can sound like a good idea for a number of reasons. For instance, it will cost less because you will need only one, or fewer, cages. You also might think it sounds fun to be able to watch more than one chameleon at a time. It would also mean that your chameleons could mate and you would end up with babies, right?

All of those reasons for having communal cages are sound... as far as they go! However, there are a number of problems with this too:

- Chameleons are solitary by nature.

- Gravid, or egg-carrying, females and shedding chameleons are even more anti-social than usual, and this can lead to stress and /or conflict between individuals.

- Smaller or weaker chameleons can be bullied and even injured by larger, more dominant chameleons.

- Females that are not sexually mature or are not receptive can become very stressed as a result of unwanted overtures from males.

- Rivalries between mature, adult chameleons of both sexes can result in fights and injuries.

All of these factors cause stress, usually of a chronic nature, and this takes a heavy toll on a chameleon's health.

Chapter 6: Buying One

1) Wild-caught versus a chameleon bred in captivity

The general consensus appears to be that a panther chameleon bred in captivity has many advantages over one that has been caught in the wild.

From the pet owner's perspective the advantages are that captive-bred chameleons are tamer as they have been handled and socialized from birth, they are hardier, less likely to have parasites, and are generally healthier.

From an environmental point of view buying a captive-bred panther chameleon from a breeder rather than an importer does not create or contribute to the demand for wild or, even worse, black market specimens. This is important in terms of the protection of the species and the sustainability of the panther chameleon in the exotic pet market.

2) Determining whether a chameleon is male or female

As indicated earlier, knowing whether a baby panther chameleon is male or female is important in terms of being able to predict the degree of care, the colorfulness, and the likely temperament of an individual chameleon. So, unless you feel confident that you can trust the dealer to accurately identify the baby's sex, it helps if you have an idea how to do so.

The first rule is not to be misled by color. When chameleons are very young both males and females can be rather drab. However, on the odd occasion you may encounter a very young female who is more colorful than the males. In other words, don't use color to determine sex.

The most important things to look for when determining a baby or adult chameleon's sex relate to body shape. While degree may

27

vary, these sex differences are present even in babies that are very recently hatched.

Males:

- The line from the stomach to along the underside of the tail is straight.

- The base of the tail is thicker in order to accommodate the sex organs that will develop as males mature.

- In older males where the sexual organs have already developed there is a bulge, called the hemipenal bulge, at the underside of the base of the tail.

- Older males also have a more developed nasal ridge, called the rostral process, which grows outwards as the chameleon matures.

Females:

- There is a slight indentation after the cloaca (or the vent out of which eggs will be laid). This indentation is found on the female's underside, just before the base of the tail.

- The base of the tail is narrower and the tail is thinner, tapering to a tip.

- There is, of course, no hemipenal bulge.

- Females have no rostral process/nasal ridge.

3) How old panther chameleons should be when they are sold

If you look for panther chameleons that are for sale, you will discover that they are sold at various ages. However, it is usually only less scrupulous breeders and importers who sell chameleons that are very young.

Selling them below the age of three months is possible, but it does not give these youngsters enough time to mature and get sufficiently strong to handle the stress and demands of transport and settling in a new enclosure. This means that these very young panther chameleons are more predisposed to stress and ill health than older specimens.

Ideally you should not buy a chameleon that is younger than three months or from a dealer that is prepared to sell panther chameleons that are younger than that.

4) How to ensure the chameleon you want is healthy

Once you have selected a specific chameleon, it's very important that you make sure that it is healthy. While it is not possible to be 100% sure, there are certain basics that you should check:

- ✓ Is it active or does it seem lethargic?

- ✓ Is it free of injuries including cuts, grazes, scratches, or lost toenails?

- ✓ Is the skin smooth? It should not be scaly. Don't confuse shedding, which is a normal occurrence, with a skin problem.

✓ Are the colors clear? Keep in mind that colors in young chameleons are muted. However, a chameleon should not look pale or colorless.

✓ Is it a healthy-looking weight? If it is very thin it could be an indication that it has parasites or that it is dehydrated. Chameleons that are underweight have slightly sunken eyes and the ribs show through in a pronounced way.

Chapter 7: What You Need to Buy for It

It is very important that you buy what you need and set up the cage before you bring your new panther chameleon home. You don't want to be setting things up once your new pet has arrived. You need to get it settled into its new home as soon as possible.

Before you buy items for your new pet it is really important to learn as much about them and their natural environment or habitat as you can. Although you will have latitude in terms of what you specifically decide to use to set up the cage or enclosure, there are

31

certain things that are non-negotiable. You also need to remember that your job is to replicate, as closely as possible, the conditions a chameleon would normally or naturally be found in.

The items you will need to invest in and set up are:

1) Cage

These days there are a number of options in terms of cages that are commercially available. You can opt for a glass vivarium or terrarium, a screen cage, or an enclosure that is a combination of glass and screen. The combination cages are also available in screen and acrylic rather than glass.

You can also get cages that don't use regular glass but rather what is called full-spectrum or low iron glass which allows more natural light, including UV rays, to penetrate the cage. This has huge health benefits for your chameleon.

Alternatively, you could build a cage yourself rather than buying one. However, this is only recommended for those who already have experience with chameleons and /or who have done a lot of careful and accurate research on the subject.

These different types of cage materials and constructions create different habitats. For instance, a glass cage will retain more heat and more moisture. With these cages the ventilation can be very poor and chameleons may suffer from respiratory problems as a result. However, glass would be a good choice in a home or climate that was either cold or dry as chameleons need humidity. On the other hand, a screen cage would be preferable in a hot, humid climate because the mesh would allow air to circulate. Too much humidity is bad for your chameleon. A reputable dealer will be able to offer advice.

An ideal cage from an owner's point of view is one that has a removable or slide-out base. This makes cleaning much easier. Furthermore, it is a good idea to buy a light or lighter-weight cage as they are easier to move and carry outside so that your chameleon can sun itself outdoors.

Some owners believe that the cage should preferably be placed above eye level. This allows your chameleon to be higher than you which mimics the height it would normally be in, in its natural habitat.

The second consideration is cage size. Some recommend a smaller cage for a baby or sub-adult (two to four months) because it is easier to watch the new chameleon and monitor how well it is settling in, eating, and drinking. Once it is older and larger (six to eight months) is should be moved into a cage big enough for an adult panther chameleon. A new arrival can be placed into an adult-sized cage straight away, but it must be monitored carefully.

Females are smaller than male panther chameleon so—in theory—they need smaller cages, even as adults. The minimum cage size for a female is considered to be about 12 inches shorter than it would be for a male, bringing the cage size to about 36"H x 24"D x 24"W or 36"H x 18"D x 18"W.

However, the size of the chameleon should not be the factor that determines cage size because females are just active as males. In fact, they are sometimes more active and need a cage that is big enough to give them more than enough space to explore and move around. The other factor that you must remember if you buy a female panther chameleon is that you need enough space in the cage for a laying bin.

The final aspect of the cage is the substrate, or the layer or substance placed at the bottom of the cage. Some owners believe that the ideal base for a chameleon cage is a bare one as other bases or substrates make cleaning more complicated, provide insects with a place to hide, and add to the problem with stagnant water standing on the cage base. So, you can arrange pot plants, branches, and vines in such a way that none of them actually rests on the floor of the cage.

If you decide you do want some sort of substrate you again have several options:

- o The simple options:

    - Newspapers or paper towels spread on the cage floor. The advantages are that they are absorbent, easy to take out and dispose of, easy to get hold of, and inexpensive.

    - A mix of sand and peat which is very absorbent and can be replaced easily.

    - Ecoearth, which is made of shredded coconut, both absorbs water and helps to provide humidity.

- o The drainage option: a bare cage bottom with drainage holes drilled in it. These holes must be cleaned out regularly as they can become blocked. This leads to water pooling on the cage floor. This water is a breeding ground for bacteria and can start to smell.

- o The complex route: if you want to plant live plants into soil at the bottom of the cage you will need a more complex drainage system which can involve drainage holes, a layer of clay, and soil. You will really need the advice of an expert here so that the plants thrive and you don't have a problem with drainage that can cause hygiene and other problems.

Regardless of the substrate you decide on it should be kept moist, but not allowed to become soggy or water-logged. If it is too wet, it can easily grow mold and become a breeding ground for bacteria.

2) Free Ranging: an alternative to a cage

Some chameleon owners prefer to free range their animals or allow them to roam freely rather than being kept in a cage. Free ranging can be an extremely fun and rewarding way to keep a panther chameleon. They often seem to enjoy the freedom, and it can make taming your pet easier. However, free ranging is not without problems, and it is not an option for a young or inexperienced owner or in an environment where there are dogs, cats, or unconfined birds.

If a chameleon is not in a cage, one has to be constantly aware of where it is as it could be anywhere in the house or apartment. If you lose track of your panther chameleon, there is the risk that it could get injured or killed as a result of being stepped on or having a run-in with an appliance.

3) Misting system

There are several reasons why a misting system of some kind is essential in your chameleon's cage. Firstly, it will be the source of water for your chameleon as they drink moisture off leaves. Water is an absolute necessity for chameleons. Secondly, it will help to create the humidity that these lizards must have in order to stay healthy. Thirdly, it will help to keep your chameleon's eyes clean. Finally, the moisture will promote the health of the live

35

plants in the cage which also, by extension, will keep your panther chameleon happy and healthy.

Many chameleon owners say that an automated misting system is essential and is a much better option than manual misting. There is a wealth of misting systems available commercially, to suit various budgets, tastes, and requirements, which are discussed in detail in a later section.

4) Plants and branches

Another crucial feature of a chameleon cage is vegetation. The majority of chameleon species spend their lives living in shrubs and trees. The panther chameleon is no exception.

You need to create an interesting habitat for your chameleon that replicates a natural one as closely as possible. If a cage is sparsely decorated, your chameleon will become stressed because of a lack of shade and hunting grounds and of boredom.

While artificial foliage is certainly easier to care for they only provide cover and shade for your chameleon. They don't hold water well, and those that aren't plastic may even absorb water. This means your chameleon may not be able to drink off the leaves, which is a very serious problem. In addition, some artificial plants contain wire in their structure which poses a hazard to your reptile. Overall, artificial plants are not recommended.

Plants have several important purposes. Firstly, they provide a sense of security and familiarity. Secondly, plant leaves are a natural surface for water droplets which the chameleon will drink from. Thirdly, the branches and vines, arranged at different angles and of varying widths, allow your chameleon to maintain and use its ability to grip and climb. Finally, they provide a place to rest, explore, and hunt.

Vegetation should consist of a range of items: plants, vines or creepers, and branches. These should preferably be live specimens, although cloth vines are fine. Plastic plants should definitely be avoided.

The plants in a chameleon's cage are very important because:

- ✓ Chameleons drink water off leaves, not out of bowls or fountains. If there are no plants, your pet will become dehydrated, which is very often fatal.

- ✓ A chameleon needs vegetation in which to explore and to enjoy. They also like to have some privacy.

- ✓ Branches and vines allow the chameleon to get around the entire cage with ease without having to climb on the screen which can damage their feet. This means that the branches and such should be arranged with care.

- ✓ Plants are the natural habitat of the panther chameleon and are therefore very important in terms of replicating their natural conditions.

- ✓ The food you provide will be live, and your chameleon will need the plants to move around on and through in order to hunt and find its food.

- ✓ Plants and vegetation help greatly to preserve the humidity your panther chameleon needs to stay healthy. In fact, some plants actually promote humidity.

The choice of plants is important too. You need to ensure that they are not toxic, that they will thrive in the cage, and not get out of control or grow too large or too fast.

You will receive good advice from a good pet retailer or a vet, but popular and safe plants for panther chameleon cages include:

o   Wax Plant (*Hoya Exotica*)
o   Dwarf Palm (*Arcca*)
o   Pothos or Hanging Devil's Ivy (*Epipremnum aureum*)
o   Hibiscus (*Hibiscus rosa-sinensis*)
o   Dwarf Umbrella (*Schefflera arboricola*)
o   Croton (*Codiaeum*)
o   Ficus (*Ficus benjamina*)

Please note, however, that the sap from some ficus plants can cause skin irritation in chameleons, so they should be used with caution despite their popularity.

A word and caution. Pesticides and insecticides are used in most plant nurseries. This means that you must prepare plants very carefully before you place them in the cage. The leaves of all plants need to be washed or wiped down very thoroughly to remove any pesticides or other potentially harmful substances or residue.

Also, when you buy potted plants, you must keep in mind that the potting soil the plant originally comes in is also likely to contain fertilizers of various kinds and soil additives that could be toxic to your chameleon. To avoid your lizard being affected by these chemical substances, you need to re-pot all the plants before you place them into the cage. Some experts recommend using a product like Supersoil which is free of potentially harmful substances and is easily available from garden centers.

38

In addition to plants and vines, your chameleon will need sturdy branches of varying thicknesses that it can use as walkways in the cage and as perches from which to spot prey. These branches should be arranged at different levels in the cage and be placed both vertically and horizontally.

You can get dead branches fairly easily, but you must make sure that they are completely clean as you don't want to expose your chameleon to chemicals or bacteria that may be on a branch.

Finally, when you have decided on the best way to arrange plants and branches you should keep the layout the same or very similar. In other words, when you clean the cage put things back as they were. Constant changes in its environment will mean your panther chameleon will have to keep adjusting, and this will cause stress.

5) Lighting

One of the essentials for the health of chameleons is ultraviolet (UVA and UVB) rays. They need them in order to synthesize vitamin D3 in their bodies. Vitamin D3 is necessary for the absorption of calcium, which, in turn, keeps their bones healthy and strong and helps with cell health.

Chameleons that are regularly exposed to UV light are more active, bask more, are more likely to reproduce, and have better appetites than those that don't get as much UV exposure.

The ideal source of these health-giving rays is, of course, natural sunlight. However, while it is a very good idea to place your chameleon outside each day—weather permitting—to be exposed to UV rays, it is essential not to let it get overheated. This can be avoided if you make sure your chameleon has shade and water.

Keep in mind that UV rays are filtered when they pass through acrylic, plastic, or ordinary window glass. This means that your panther chameleon won't be getting these health-giving rays if its cage is made of materials that block or filter out most of them.

Of course you need to make sure that your chameleon is getting UV light inside its cage too. An ultraviolet light source such as a UV bulb should be kept on for between 10 and 12 hours each day to ensure your lizard gets enough UV exposure. These bulbs usually last for about six months.

Special basking bulbs are also available. These bulbs will create that hot-spot your chameleon needs to raise its body temperature if it starts to drop too low. It's useful to keep in mind that a burning 60 watt bulb will generate approximately 82 degrees Fahrenheit or 28 degrees Centigrade.

On a final note, it has been discovered that chameleons are able to regulate their own body temperature and their exposure to UV rays without help from us! This means that you need to provide heat and UV light separately. Neither of these heat and light sources should be closer that 8 inches or 20 centimeters from the nearest perch to avoid burns.

6) Heating

Like other reptiles, chameleons are exothermic. In other words, they need external heat or heat in and from the environment in order to stay healthy and active. Heat is also what helps them to digest their food and maintain a strong immune system.

Panther chameleons have specific requirements in terms of temperature ranges. The temperature in the cage generally should be between 75 and 90 degrees Fahrenheit or 24 to 32 degrees Centigrade during the day. The night temperature ranges should be approximately 10 to 15 degrees Fahrenheit or 5 to 10 degrees Centigrade lower than the daytime temperature.

In addition to the general gradient temperature, you need to have a basking spot in the cage. The temperature in this area should be about 10 to 15 degrees Fahrenheit, or 5 to 10 degrees Centigrade, higher than the usual daytime temperature range. It is also necessary to adjust the temperature of the basking spot to accommodate seasonal changes. This can be achieved by using bulbs with higher or lower wattage or by moving the bulb closer to or further away from the basking spot.

All heating sources, whether they are bulbs or ceramic heating elements, must be placed with great care so that they are not where your panther chameleon can burn itself or become too hot.

The temperatures throughout the cage should vary. The general rule is that the temperature should be higher near the top of the cage and at the basking site and lower at the center and base of the cage. This allows the chameleon to move around and adjust its own body temperature as necessary.

7) Misting system options

Why these systems are essential

Chameleons can manage without food for a couple of days without suffering serious ill effects. However, this is not true of water. Daily hydration is essential for a chameleon's health, and they get their water off leaves, not from water bowls or some other kind of container.

In addition to providing the necessary water drops on leaves for drinking purposes, misting also helps to maintain the necessary levels of humidity in the cage. Panther chameleons require

41

humidity levels of between 60% and 85% to be comfortable and healthy. That is impossible without enough water in the cage.

You may also want to consider buying a hygrometer to measure humidity levels so you can adjust them if necessary. It is very difficult to accurately estimate or guess at humidity levels, and you need to get them right in order to keep your chameleon healthy.

The first choice you need to make is between an automated system of some kind and a manual one. Manual systems may consist of either a spray bottle or a pressurized sprayer. Some chameleon owners enjoy spraying their panther chameleon's cage themselves. This does have some serious drawbacks, although, of course, a manual system will cost less.

However, for those that want an automated system there are several options:

Automated Misting systems

Misting Systems:

Misting systems force water through some kind of special head that creates a very fine mist which lands over a wide area including on the surfaces of the leaves of the plants in your panther chameleon's cage. The spray collects and forms droplets that a chameleon can drink and that also make their way down to the roots of the plants in the cage. In addition, the mist helps maintain the necessary humidity in the cage.

There are a number of automated or automatic misting systems available commercially. The number and variety can be a little confusing, so it would be a good idea to get some advice from a reputable chameleon breeder, an experienced panther chameleon owner, or a vet.

42

The primary advantages of these systems is that you can set them to run at regular times each day so that you establish a routine for your chameleon—which it will thrive on—and so that it will get the water and hydration it needs whether you are there or not. It also means that if you have to be away you don't have to ask the sitter to spray your pet chameleon/s.

The disadvantage is that these systems can be a little too efficient and cause flooding or water to pool around the cage.

This means that a drainage and water collection system is also a must-have. Here, again, you could have a pretty simple system such as drainage holes in the bottom of the cage with buckets to catch the water or a more sophisticated system of drains.

Rain systems:

These are very similar to misting systems except that instead of a fine spray these systems deliver larger drips of water from a series of little holes in a network of tubing above the cage.

How much water falls will depend on the number of tubes used and how many holes there are in each tube. It is important that the rain not lead to a flood!

Drip systems:

These are perhaps the most popular systems with owners. They are similar to rain systems, but there are far fewer drops and they emerge more slowly—hence the name drip—from the ends of a more limited number of pipes. One of the main advantages of this gravity-fed system is that you are less likely to have to deal with flooding or a lot of water splashing or running outside of the cage.

Manual Misting

Some panther chameleon owners prefer to water their pet lizards manually once or twice a day using a spray bottle or a high pressure spray-gun. If you only have one or two chameleons, are disciplined, and you are at home every day, this can work well.

However, this is not a good idea if you are away often, have to rely on somebody to do it for you, or have several chameleons. As indicated, these reptiles need a schedule and daily hydration. If they don't get water at regular intervals every day, they will become ill. Using a manual system to spray more than one cage can be time consuming and very hard on one's hands! In addition, because hydration is so essential to your chameleon's survival, you can't decide you are too tired or just don't feel like doing it.

Automated versus manual systems

When it comes to lighting and misting systems automation can be a huge advantage for both you and your panther chameleon. In addition to using automated systems rather than manual ones, it is a very good idea to connect timers to them.

If you have this kind of set-up, you will create a routine and a predictable environment for your chameleon because light and water will come on and go off at set times every day. This will have emotional and physical benefits for him or her.

It also offers major benefits for you because you can be confident in the knowledge that your panther chameleon will be at the right temperature and have the water it needs even if you are out, away, or just running later than expected or anticipated. It can be much easier to rely on this kind of infrastructure than having to ask family or friends to cover for you.

8) Vitamin supplements

This is a controversial topic up to a point. What is agreed on is that both a vitamin and calcium supplement should be given to captive chameleons. What is not always agreed on is how much is necessary and the frequency with which it should be given.

One factor that will affect the "how much" and "how often" questions is the products or supplements that you use. It must be remembered that supplements are given to a chameleon in addition to a varied and healthy diet. Chameleons should, of course, ideally get the right nutrition through the foods they are given to eat.

Perhaps a good guideline is that when you dust food insects with a supplement you do so lightly.

A further factor that will affect how often and how much you need to dose your pet with supplements is the age and state of health or condition of the chameleon. Panther chameleons have higher metabolism rates that some other species so they can tolerate slightly more supplements than other types of chameleon.

Generally, consensus is that vitamin supplements are necessary even if your chameleon is being fed properly and getting enough UV exposure. They all help to create the right balance in a chameleon's body.

Equally important is ensuring that the right amount of each vitamin is given to your panther chameleon or the balance in its body will be upset. The vitamins that are needed are:

✓ *Calcium*: Most people associate calcium with healthy bones and teeth, but that's only part of the picture. This mineral is necessary for the majority of systems in the chameleon's body, including muscles.

If a reptile doesn't get enough calcium, it will start to draw the mineral from its own bones. This in turn leads to serious conditions. These will be discussed in more detail in chapter 10 of this guide.

✓ *Phosphorous*: This important mineral is found naturally in bones and other cells. Its primary function is the regulation of the body's use of other minerals and vitamins. The levels of calcium and phosphorous need to mirror and balance each other or the animal becomes weakened or ill.

Calcium and phosphorous actually work together, but too much of one will block the absorption of the other. The diet of pet or captive chameleons can cause an imbalance; how to avoid this or deal with it will be discussed in chapter 9.

✓ *Vitamin D3*: This vitamin is also known as the "sunshine vitamin" as animals can naturally synthesize vitamin D3 in their skin if they are exposed to sunlight. Vitamin D3 is essential for calcium absorption in bones.

While other animals can get this vitamin from food, reptiles like panther chameleons rely on basking in the sun or UV light in order to produce most of the D3 they need.

In addition to making bones stronger, this important vitamin is necessary for a strong immune system. Furthermore, it helps to maintain the correct or healthy levels of calcium and phosphorous in the blood.

✓ *Vitamin A*: While your chameleon needs it for eye, bone, cells, and immune system health, this is one of the vitamins a creature can have too much of. The consequences of too much vitamin A or a toxic level of this vitamin are serious as the muscles and nerves are affected.

In severe cases, a vitamin A overdose or toxicity affects calcium levels in the kidneys, liver, and muscles and will weaken bones.

The bottom line with vitamins is that it is crucial to maintain the right balance in your panther chameleon's body and systems.

How to contribute to this balance will be discussed further in relation to what you feed your chameleon and with gut loading the insects that you give your chameleon.

Chapter 8: Handling & Caring for It

1) Handling your chameleon

It is certainly true that some reptiles don't enjoy being handled. Chameleons in particular become stressed if they are handled, and the odd, more aggressive individual may even bite.

However, each panther chameleon has a different personality, and some are a lot friendlier, more laid-back, and relaxed than others. Some owners have taught their chameleons to tolerate being handled for brief periods, and there are steps you can take to "tame" your lizard:

- Don't start immediately; *give your new chameleon a chance to settle* into its new environment. They will arrive stressed and unsettled and being handled by you will add to this. A new arrival must have time to explore their cage and get used to it and the new routines in terms of water, light, and feeding. It is suggested that you make no attempt to handle a new chameleon for the first week or even two weeks.

- Food will be your great ally when getting your panther chameleon used to you. By *hand-feeding your new pet* you will get it used to being near your hand and, by extension, near you. If you can get your chameleon to associate something good with you, namely food, it is less likely to feel fear when you are close.

You don't need to take "hand-feeding" too literally. The prey or food item can be held with tweezers, for example, if you don't want to touch it. You need to hold the food out to your panther chameleon and wait till it shoots its tongue out to take it. To reduce the length of the wait it can be a good idea to do this for the first feed of the day when a chameleon is at its hungriest.

Even so, your pet will be nervous at first. For this reason don't put your hand too close and don't watch or stare at your chameleon; try to be relaxed and nonchalant about it. Don't try to force things or hurry them up. You need to rely on the wriggling food to get the lizard's attention and prompt it to take aim and shoot out its tongue.

Finally, don't expect to have success the first time you try this. Some chameleon owners do, but it is unlikely. It may not even work on day two, three, four, or five. With chameleons that are more nervous by nature it may take weeks. But you need to persevere because eventually your panther chameleon will take food from you.

49

Hand feeding is the essential first step in getting your pet used to you and being around you. Without it you won't have much luck taming your chameleon.

- The next step is to *get your panther chameleon out of its cage*. Don't reach in, grab your chameleon, and take it out of the cage. You need to open the door and let it come out when it is ready and you are in the room. Even if you think you will be gentle, you need to look at it from your pet's perspective. If you were a caged chameleon and a large hand was reaching for you, you would also get really stressed and /or aggressive.

Leave the cage door open and place a potted plant in front of it. Ignore your chameleon, but stay in the room and do something else. It may take hours before your chameleon is brave or confident enough to leave the cage. Eventually it will, though, as curiosity will get the better of it and it will feel less anxious.

Each day you try this, your chameleon will leave its cage sooner. Once it is comfortable in the plant in front of the cage, you can place your hand slowly, palm up, in front of your colorful lizard. If it takes this calmly, you can pick it up and let it walk on your hand for a minute or so. Then return it to the plant.

Each time you handle your panther chameleon you can do so for a slightly longer time. With this stage, as with the others, you must be patient and be restrained. If you do too much too soon you may be back at square one and your chameleon may not want to risk it again.

This way you build up trust gradually and your chameleon becomes increasingly used to you. Eventually you will be able to place your hand in the cage and your chameleon will walk onto it.

- You need to *make sure that your chameleon associates being out of its cage and being handled by you with positive or enjoyable consequences.* For example, in addition to hand-feeding you could give your anther chameleon time to bask in natural light outside or wander around and explore potted plants in your room but outside the cage. If you do this, your lizard will have an, "Oh good!" reaction rather than getting stressed when you remove it from its cage.

- Although many chameleons will learn to tolerate, or even enjoy, being out and handled you need to *pay attention to your individual pet.* Some are just way more timid and anxious than others, and may only get as far as nervously eating from your hand. Others will be sociable and enthusiastic and may even approach the cage door when they see you. If you observe stressed or aggressive behavior, such as gaping or hissing, you need to back up and be patient.

  The bottom line is that you need to be patient, use rewards to reinforce the behavior you want, pay attention to your chameleon's signals, don't handle any chameleon for too long, and respect their needs and space.

This process takes a lot of time and patience. However, it is really worth it because it makes your panther chameleon a more fun pet for you, and it makes life more interesting for your chameleon. A further benefit is that a chameleon that is able to tolerate being handled is much easier to deal with and treat if it is ill and needs to be seen by the vet.

A final tip is that when you handle your panther chameleon you shouldn't restrain it by holding it. Ideally, you should let it walk on you and move from one hand to the other. Because they like being high up don't be surprised if your chameleon tries to climb up your arms and onto your head! If you need to move or pick up your chameleon remember to do so extremely gently and not to touch its back or take hold of it by the tail.

2) Cleaning your panther chameleon's cage

The high temperatures and humidity levels in a chameleon cage, combined with the unavoidable insect and fecal matter and sometimes some stagnant water, mean that it is heaven on earth for the types of bacteria and even parasites that breed in these types of conditions. All of these organisms pose a serious risk to the health of your chameleon, so cleaning the cage regularly and thoroughly is essential. It also prevents the cage from smelling.

It's strongly recommended that you do a quick clean daily. This cleaning should involve removing insect matter, pieces of shed skin, fecal matter, and any water at the bottom of the cage that hasn't drained away properly. You can also remove leaves or parts of leaves that have waste matter stuck to them. You can use a pair of scissors for this to carefully cut off or out the affected section of a leaf. This is effective from a hygiene point of view and shouldn't affect the health of the plant. If you do this basic cleaning every day it will make the weekly or the bi-monthly cleaning less daunting.

A big clean is necessary in order to make sure that all of the surfaces of the cage and pieces of equipment, such as light fittings, are truly clean and free of bacteria, etc. The breeder or dealer you buy your panther chameleon from (or your vet) can advise about the best cleaning solutions to use. Some standard household cleaning products should be avoided as they contain chemicals that will be toxic to your chameleon.

There are a number of things to remember when you carry out a thorough cleaning of your chameleon's cage:

o   You must, of course, remove your chameleon from the cage first so that it is not stressed and or exposed to cleaning solutions or at risk of injury. Place it where it is out of the way and safe while you work.

o   If you use a manual watering system don't use the same spray or pressure bottle for the cleaning solution as you do for the water. If you do you run the risk of contaminating the water even if you rinse the bottle afterwards.

    The big danger is that you will get some chemical solution on your chameleon the next time that you spray water into the cage. If you use separate bottles make sure that you label them to prevent confusion or a mix-up.

o   Don't spray cleaning solution onto the leaves of live plants as it may burn them. In addition it will leave a chemical residue on the leaves that your chameleon will be exposed to when it brushes past them or drinks drops of water off them.

o   Once you have sprayed the surfaces of the cage and removed the dirt and waste material you need to carefully wipe up the excess cleaning material. You then must rinse all the surfaces very thoroughly. Again, this is to make sure that your chameleon isn't exposed to any cleaning solution or toxins.

o Finish the cleaning process by drying the rinsed surfaces carefully and thoroughly with a cloth that is not going to leave threads or fluff in the cage that could pose a danger to your pet. You also don't want to leave any extra water lying around as this, too, is not hygienic.

Chapter 9: Feeding It

1) What & how often to feed your chameleon

What to feed your panther chameleon

Panther chameleons, like the majority of chameleons, are insectivores and therefore need to be given a diet consisting of a wide variety of insects and worms. A varied and balanced diet will result in a healthy and happy pet.

Staple insects for daily feeding for chameleons include crickets, roaches/cockroaches, silkworms, and super worms. Crickets and silkworms are the most popular with breeders and owners and are recommended by those experienced with chameleons more often than any other staple foods (feeders). Both of these insects and other commonly used foods such as flies, grasshoppers, wax worms, butter worms, meal worms, and horn worms are all commercially available.

Butter worms are high in calcium. While calcium is essential for panther chameleons, too much is problematic; butter worms are a treat, not a staple. Mealworms, wax worms, and super worms should also only be used in limited quantities as these worms are very high in fat.

You may also find that your panther chameleon enjoys some plant matter too. You could try your chameleon on:

- Turnip greens
- Romaine lettuce
- Mustard Greens
- Broccoli
- Sugar snap peas
- Collard Greens
- Kale leaves
- Slices of orange

- Carrots
- Alfalfa
- Yams
- Yellow Squash
- Zucchini
- Apple skins
- Potato peelings
- Banana skins.

Some breeders suggest that one should give a chameleon plant material or greens of some sort once or twice a week.

Regardless of what you feed your pet you must monitor its intake. If there are food items it never eats, leave them out. If your lizard doesn't eat all the insects that you put out at feeding times, or seems to be getting a little fat, you need to feed it less.

What not to feed your chameleon

You need to avoid giving your lizard fireflies as they contain a substance that is toxic to chameleons. In addition, wild-caught insects should not be used because they may have been exposed to pesticides and insecticides that will be poisonous to your panther chameleon when it ingests the substances along with the insect.

It's also vital that you don't leave uneaten live food in the cage for long periods. These insects can become contaminated. For instance, some of them are likely to eat fecal matter. The most serious possibility is that some insects may actually attack your chameleon!

A further "don't" is buying insects from pet store feeders as they may not be clean or well maintained. Crickets are particularly susceptible to contamination of this kind. You need to buy food for your chameleon that is clean and free of bacteria and parasites.

Feeding methods

In addition to food types, you will also need to decide about the feeding method you want to use. You can opt for either cup feeding or what is called free-roaming feeding. With cup feeding a container of food is placed in the cage and the chameleon can then eat the insects or worms from the container when it wants to. Free-roaming means that live insects are released into the cage and the chameleon hunts them. Both methods have advantages and disadvantages.

Cup feeding:

The advantages of cup feeding are that the container keeps the food in one place, prevents it from getting out, and also means that meal times are quick because the chameleon doesn't need to look for the food as it is all in one place.

On the down side, not all food types can be contained in a feeding cup. For example, flies, ants, and some worms will get out of the cup with great ease. This might mean that the types of food used are therefore a little more limited. In addition, your chameleon could get bored with the same routine. Finally, and of most concern, cup-fed chameleons can develop problems with their tongues. If this is serious enough, it can prevent the chameleon from eating and it will starve.

Free roaming:

The most obvious advantage of free-roaming feeding is that this method most closely replicates the natural way of feeding for chameleons: looking for and catching prey in the plants. It also means that your panther chameleon has to hunt and it is therefore kept active. Lastly, it's much better exercise for its tongue.

The negatives are that live food that is left in the cage and is not eaten by the chameleon can cause problems. They can escape from the cage, go into hiding, or eat the chameleon's feces and become contaminated. If a contaminated insect is then eaten by your chameleon, the chameleon will become ill. Also, some insects may even attack a chameleon if the insect is left in the cage for too long.

Food and supplements

Calcium and phosphorous:

Because crickets and some other insects contain high quantities of phosphorous, it's essential to supplement with a phosphorous-free calcium powder at most feedings (especially if your chameleon is being fed crickets). You also need to provide some calcium-rich insects such as butter worms and phoenix worms.

It is really important that the calcium to phosphorous ratio in the chameleon's body is balanced at all times. However, if one of these minerals is too high, it's much better if it's the calcium rather than the phosphorous as that will have fewer adverse effects on the lizard's health.

These minerals, the necessary balances, and how to try to achieve and maintain them in your panther chameleon are discussed in a later section in relation to feeding, food types, and signs to watch out for.

Vitamin D3:

If you give your panther chameleon enough exposure to natural sunlight, and you have a UV light on in the cage that burns for enough hours during each day, your chameleon will naturally produce all the vitamin D3 that it needs.

Vitamin A:

You can get vitamin A in two different forms. The first is found in animal sources and is called preformed vitamin A. The other form is known as beta-carotenoids. This latter type is found in plants, especially in dark green and orange vegetables and fruits.

In order to feed your panther chameleon preformed vitamin A, you need to gut load the insects and worms with food stuffs such as liver, eggs, dairy, and some types of cereals. In other words, you feed these to your chameleon's food and then your pet will receive the benefits when it eats the insects that are high in vitamin A thanks to the gut loading!

Alternatively, you could buy a vitamin A supplement from a pet store or your vet.

Variety in your chameleon's diet

Variety is necessary not just because it makes meal-times more fun and less boring for your pet (and you) but also because it is more likely to help you provide the necessary vitamins and minerals for your chameleon!

The more variety there is in terms of the insects and plant matter that you feed your panther chameleon, the better. In addition, the more varied the foodstuffs that you feed your chameleon's food the better! This variety ensures that your pet receives all the nutrients that it needs to be healthy and that those nutrients are in the correct balance in its body.

2) Caring for & feeding your chameleon's food

What to feed your chameleon's food

The term "gut loading" has already been introduced, but one needs to look more closely at it. Gut loading is feeding food to your chameleon's food before you feed it to your chameleon. In other words, to feed your panther chameleon well you need to feed the insects and worms it will eat well so they are strong, clean, and nutritious. It also sometimes involves dusting insects with a supplement as a way to get your chameleon to ingest the vitamins and minerals that it needs.

So, your chameleon's food needs to be gut loaded. You can either collect food for the crickets, worms, etc. you have or you can buy dry gut loading mix. Along with foods such as cereals, eggs, liver, and plant materials, your chameleon's food must be given water. The water is usually contained in the food you feed them.

By gut loading you make sure that the food—whatever form it takes—contains the nutrients that your panther chameleon needs and that the insects' and worms' systems are flushed out and clean. This also means that the food items you feed to the insects must be clean too!

In addition, certain feeders have specific requirements when it comes to their diet:

- Silkworms require specific types of leaves such as freshly picked and washed mulberry or beetroot leaves.

- Super worms and meal worms must have bran or oats and water in the form of carrots or other vegetables.

- Wax worms and butter worms are treats for your pet rather than regular food. They are plant-specific feeders, so it's better to get small quantities of these worms from a reputable vet shop. They also need plant matter and water.

- Flies are sold along with a food culture that contains all the things that they need so that you don't have to do anything.

How to house your panther chameleon's food

Generally your chameleon's food should be kept at between 70 to 80 degrees Fahrenheit or 21 to 27 degrees Centigrade. There may be some variations and you can get more species-specific information from the retailer or individual that you buy the food from.

- ➢ *Flies, butter worms, wax worms, and horn worms*: These are usually sold in cups which are just fine to keep them in. In other words, no special containers are required for them.

- ➢ *Meal worms*: These worms should be kept in the cups they come in, in the refrigerator to slow down their growth. They grow, mature, and die quickly so you want to slow down this process rather than losing most of these worms.

- ➢ *Crickets*: Most suppliers sell crickets in batches of 1000 eggs. The crickets should be housed in a large container that stands vertically.

  Some chameleon owners use barrels or large bins for this purpose. However, the opening of the container that you use must be covered with a metal screen so the crickets can't chew their way out. Aluminum is a good choice for this purpose.

➤ *Super worms*: These worms require a tub or plastic box that holds their bedding and keeps them from crawling out. They are very active and large worms, but a simple plastic box with a screen top lid is pretty effective.

It's also very important that they have enough space and water-carrying food or they will cannibalize or eat each other.

➤ *Silkworms*: A dry, warm environment is required for these worms. Large or medium-sized cardboard boxes work well as these worms are fairly sedentary. Plastic tubs are less successful for housing silkworms perhaps because it becomes too warm for them. The optimal container is, not surprisingly, a silkworm keeper which can be bought at a retailer or online.

➤ *Roaches/cockroaches*: You need to know what type of roach you have bought as you can get climbing and non-climbing roaches. If they are non-climbing roaches, you can use an ordinary tub or a box to keep them in.

However, climbing roaches need special arrangements so they can't get out of the container. One simple way to prevent them getting out is to (a) use a higher container than for the non-climbing roaches and (b) smear some Vaseline below and around the rim of the container so that they won't be able to get purchase on the sides and will slide or drop down into the container.

3) Water

Panther chameleons don't drink from bowls or drinking fountains the way many pets do, including some reptiles. However, it is essential that you ensure that your chameleon gets enough water. Dehydration will most certainly result first in kidney failure and later in death.

In the wild, chameleons drink water from dew or rain drops that collect on leaves. You need to replicate that in their cage. This is, as touched on earlier, where misting and other water systems come in. You must introduce water through your chosen system at least three times a day.

In addition to providing the water droplets on leaves that your chameleon needs, this process also keeps the humidity at the level it needs to be.

And a final word or two of caution:

- If you use a manual system to deliver water to your chameleon or chameleons do not forget to spray several times a day. You can't decide it won't matter if you skip one or two or you just don't feel like doing it. Your poor memory or laziness will cost your chameleon its life!

- Don't use a waterfall as a water delivery system. Firstly, your panther chameleon is unlikely to drink from it. Secondly, it can very easily become contaminated by fecal matter or insect matter. What's more, waterfalls are hard to clean and therefore pose a definite health risk to your chameleon.

- Don't ever spray water directly onto your chameleon, especially onto its face, as this can lead to eye problems, including eye infections.

Chapter 10: Its Health and Yours

1) Shedding

What is shedding?

Reptiles grow very rapidly during the early stages, or the first six to nine months, of their lives. Their skin doesn't accommodate this growth so they have to shed the old skin that has become too small to accommodate their increased body size.

The formal term for shedding is ecdysis. Most lizards, including the panther chameleon, shed their skin in pieces or sections and not in a single piece the way snakes do.

How often panther chameleons shed

As indicated, while your chameleon is under a year of age it will grow fast. This means that it will, on average, shed its skin about every two to three weeks.

Once it is an adult, a panther chameleon sheds less often. There is no hard and fast rule. Some chameleons shed monthly, whereas others only shed every two or three months.

Pre-shedding behavior

Some chameleon owners, especially first-time owners, become very concerned about their pet the first time they are getting ready to shed because pre-shedding behavior can be confused with signs of ill health.

A panther chameleon that is about to shed can get really cranky. Even chameleons that are normally docile may become aggressive or at least very bad tempered. An ordinarily sociable reptile that is about to shed is unlikely to want to be handled.

You may also notice that your chameleon is duller in color than usual. In addition, you may observe white or gray spots or patches on the chameleon's head and back a day or two before the shed begins in earnest.

Finally, a chameleon that is about to shed will have a greatly reduced appetite. It may even stop eating altogether.

Shedding behavior

Shedding appears to be a necessary, but uncomfortable and even unpleasant process for reptiles. Once the shedding has begun your chameleon will probably still eat much less than usual or not eat at all. It will also continue to feel grumpy and anti-social, so you should avoid handling it unless it is absolutely essential. You need to just give your pet some space and time to get through the shed.

Most panther chameleons shed fairly quickly (usually within 24 hours) and will arch their backs and shake themselves in order to speed the process up. However, shedding can take a few days with some individuals. The shed skin comes off in sections until it has all been shed with the skin on the feet and head sometimes being the last pieces to come loose.

How to care for a shedding chameleon

Usually your chameleon should be able to manage the process without any help at all from you. What can be helpful for it, however, is if you slightly increase the amount of water or the humidity levels in the cage as this softens the skin. This makes it easier for your panther chameleon to get rid of the old skin.

A problem shed and what to do about it

If your chameleon does not shed completely, you need to be concerned about the health of your pet because this is usually due to an underlying and perhaps serious issue. Dysecdysis, or incomplete or problem shedding, will happen again and again unless you find out why your panther chameleon is having difficulty. Some common causes include:

- Illness of some sort

- Insufficient humidity in the cage

- A diet that lacks the necessary nutrients

67

- Stress

- Being handled too much during the shedding phase

- Problems with housing or its habitat which could include lighting conditions and temperature

- A lack of branches or other surfaces to rub or brush against that help a chameleon to dislodge the old skin.

Naturally you will want to do what you can to help your panther chameleon with its shedding. However, if you try to pull off the pieces of old skin still sticking to a chameleon you need to do so extremely gently. Pieces that don't come off in response to very gentle pressure should not be pulled at further or harder.

If you pull or tear bits of skin off before they are ready to come off you can easily damage the new and only partly formed skin or scales underneath. Not only will this cause your chameleon pain but it will leave it at risk of infection and also mites.

If your lizard is having a problem shed and you notice that there are rings of old skin around its toes or any other parts of its extremities you do need to intervene. These pieces are worrying because they can cut off or restrict blood flow in the limb or digits with serious results including, potentially, conditions that will lead to the need to amputate toes.

The way to remove this problematic old skin is to soak it in water until it is soft enough to remove. If you are concerned or feel unable to do this yourself, take your panther chameleon to your vet who will be able to do it for you.

2) General early signs of illness

Chameleons don't show the symptoms of illness early on as part of an instinctive survival technique. In the wild, a sick animal is far more likely to become a meal so the panther chameleon masks symptoms in order to protect itself. As a result, you will have to get to know your panther chameleon as quickly as possible and observe it every day so that you can immediately pick up if it is off-color or unwell.

Early detection of problems is essential. A chameleon that is thin, pale, has sunken or closed eyes, and has a weak grip may well already be past help, even from a vet.

3) Common Chameleon illnesses and health problems

Cuts and wounds:

It is not unusual for chameleons to suffer minor wounds or small, superficial cuts. If you are sure that the cut or wound is neither deep nor infected this is a medical situation that you can treat yourself.

You need to keep the wound clean and apply a topical cream such as *Vetericyn HydroGel* that cleans the wound and kills bacteria. You can buy this product, or a similar one, from a retailer or from your vet.

Parasites:

Wild-caught chameleons often carry what is called a heavy parasite load. In other words they will have several types of internal and/or external parasite. On the other hand, captive-born chameleons can pick up parasites from their food, as a result of poor cage hygiene, from contaminated water sources, or even as a result of contact with reptiles that have parasites.

For this reason you need to have fecal exams done by the vet from time to time to make sure that your panther chameleon does not have parasites. Some owners are of the opinion that these tests should be done every quarter. This is especially crucial if wild insects are part of your chameleon's diet.

It's unusual to find wild-caught chameleons that don't have at least one type of internal parasite. The stress of capture and the captivity, transportation, etc. that follows can actually cause an increase in parasite numbers in the chameleon's body. If a wild-caught chameleon is badly weakened by the stress of the whole capture process, an anti-parasite drug can kill it as the parasites can migrate to organs such as the lungs.

As the owner of a chameleon you shouldn't necessarily trust that when a retailer or importer tells you that a panther chameleon is free of parasites that this is actually the case. You would be well advised to take your new pet to a vet for tests to confirm or discount the presence of parasites and, if there are some, identify the type so they can be treated quickly and effectively.

Don't just go ahead and give a new chameleon an anti-parasite treatment unless you know the extent of the problem and the type of parasite you are dealing with. A vet will do laboratory tests on blood, stool, and sputum samples. A specific treatment will be prescribed based on the findings. Follow-up tests will be needed to make sure the treatment was effective and that all the parasites have been eliminated.

You should also watch your chameleon for any signs or symptoms of parasite infestation: feces that smell really bad (with chameleons the fecal matter normally has no odor at all), loose or watery stools, or feces that contain blood, mucus, or undigested food. If you notice any of these signs it's time to visit the vet!

Metabolic Bone Disease:

Metabolic Bone Disease or MBD is the most common condition in young chameleons. In sub-adults the disease is called rickets. This condition is the result of vitamin and mineral deficiencies or the opposite: too much of a vitamin or mineral. If there is too little or too much vitamin D3, vitamin A, calcium, or phosphorous in a chameleon's system it may well develop this horrible disease.

In chameleons with MBD the bones become very thin and weak and, as a result, they either bend or break. This applies to the bones in their limbs and tails, the ribs, and other bones. One can actually see some of the effects: bowed front legs, kinked tails, deformed backs, infirm or "wobbly" jaws, and a lack of coordination when they walk or climb. MBD and rickets can also cause kidney damage and destroy the chameleon's ability to walk, perch on a branch, drink, or eat as the tongue no longer functions properly.

This is a very painful condition and death comes slowly, but is inevitable. It is also very distressing to watch for a caring owner. If you suspect your panther chameleon has rickets or MBD, take it to the vet immediately.

The best way to prevent this awful disease is to make sure that your chameleon gets regular exposure to natural light and UV rays as this promotes the production of vitamin D3, which is essential for the absorption of other minerals and vitamins.

Lack of sunlight and therefore vitamin D3 and calcium:

If a chameleon doesn't get enough exposure to natural sunlight and enough time under a UV bulb, it won't be able to produce any vitamin D3. Chameleons naturally produce this essential vitamin when they have the UV conditions that they need.

Without vitamin D3 in their bodies, chameleons aren't able to absorb the calcium present in their food. The absence of calcium, as discussed in more detail in chapter 7 under the section on supplements, causes serious health problems in all reptiles including panther chameleons.

However, while natural sunlight is vital, it can also pose a risk. If your chameleon is overexposed to UV rays it can suffer thermal burns or what is often called sunburn. It is therefore important that you don't leave your chameleon in the sun for too long.

If you are concerned that your chameleon's environment doesn't provide enough sunlight, and that it might be suffering from a vitamin D3 deficiency as a result, you can buy vitamin D3 in liquid or powder form, and you can use this as part of gut loading your chameleon's food.

Dehydration:

Dehydration is a very serious medical condition in all creatures, and chameleons are no exception. In fact, many animals can go much longer without food than they can without water. If your panther chameleon is not receiving the drinking water it needs, you are going to have an unwell and eventually a dead chameleon on your hands. There is no excuse for allowing a chameleon to become dehydrated. How much or how little water a chameleon gets depends entirely on you. There are several issues that can lead to dehydration.

72

A watering system that is inefficient or erratic will contribute to dehydration. Manual watering that is not thorough or regular enough is often a culprit too. The humidity in the cage is also not a substitute for a misting (or other water delivery) system. There must be water on leaves at regular intervals that your chameleon can drink. These are all factors that an owner is responsible for and can correct before they adversely affect the chameleon's well-being and health.

What makes dehydration even more dangerous is that the early signs of this condition in chameleons are not easy to spot. However, once a chameleon is already dehydrated the symptoms are very clear and dramatic. These symptoms include lethargy or inactivity, a total loss of appetite, and very sunken eyes. Usually a chameleon that has reached this stage can't be treated even by a vet and death will inevitably follow.

Kidney Failure:

Kidney failure is a leading cause of death in pet chameleons and it is usually the result of chronic dehydration. This can be the case even if the dehydration is low-level. Over time slight but chronic dehydration places a strain on the kidneys. They then stop functioning properly and subsequently they will fail completely.

The second cause of kidney failure in captive chameleons is linked to the administration of antibiotics that are toxic for the kidneys. Some of these antibiotics are used in the treatment of bacterial infections. Your vet can monitor kidney function through blood tests if it is necessary to give your chameleon antibiotics that have the potential to cause kidney problems.

Acidosis:

Acidosis is characterized by low pH in body tissues and blood. In other words, the blood and tissues become too acidic. This causes lactates to build up in the tissues, and this can cause extreme stiffness and lethargy.

Reptiles, chameleons included, are especially prone to this condition because of the nature of their metabolisms. Although this problem is less of a risk for chameleons than it is for other reptiles that put in sudden bursts of activity, it can still be a problem that a vet would need to diagnose and treat. It must be treated as soon as possible.

Alkalosis:

Alkalosis is at the opposite end of the spectrum because with this condition the pH levels are too high and the blood is therefore very alkaline. This is usually accompanied by low levels of potassium and/or calcium in the blood and tissues. This condition causes muscle problems: pain, weakness, and spasms. Your vet would be able to diagnose and treat this condition if it was noticed early enough.

Gout:

Gout is a painful condition caused when uric acid in the blood forms tiny, sharp crystals that lodge in joints and cause swelling and inflammation. Gout may be a by-product of kidney problems because if they are not functioning properly, they are not able to clean the blood properly.

A panther chameleon suffering from gout may have visibly swollen joints, such as the knees, or may dangle a back leg while perching in order to ease the pressure on the joints in the leg and so relieve the pain in them. The pain may mean that the chameleon is reluctant to move about, which can also lead to problems.

A vet will make a diagnosis of gout after performing blood tests to examine uric acid levels and taking x-rays.

Maladaptation to captivity:

Panther chameleons that are born in captivity will, of course, not suffer from this problem. Only wild-caught chameleons are susceptible to this condition, which is not so much a physical one as an emotional and behavioral one. This does, of course, impact on the physical health of the chameleon too.

This syndrome is thought to be caused by the marked and chronic stress brought about by their capture, resultant loss of freedom, the daily interaction with people following being captured, transportation, and having to adjust to being caged.

Signs of this condition include not eating, aggression, pacing the enclosure, head-butting the sides of the cage, pallor or poor levels of color, lethargy, and depression.

In some cases providing extra plants and cover in the cage can ease this condition. However, in other wild-caught chameleons there is no improvement, and their immune systems become so weakened from the stress that they die from illnesses they may otherwise not have caught.

Stress:

The majority of chameleons experience some degree of captivity-related stress. Chronic stress damages or suppresses the immune system, and without a strong immune system animals become ill.

In the case of chameleons, a compromised immune system means they are more vulnerable to parasites, increased numbers of parasites, and bacterial infections of various kinds.

Fortunately there are things a panther chameleon owner can do to reduce stress in their pet:

✓ Don't move quickly near your chameleon.

✓ Place the cage in a quiet, low traffic area.

✓ Don't keep more than one chameleon in a cage.

✓ Ensure that pets, such as dogs and cats, don't go near, sniff, or scratch at the chameleon's cage.

✓ Keep other pets that are natural predators (snakes, large birds, etc.) where your chameleon can't see them.

✓ Don't have any surfaces that will allow your chameleon to see its own reflection, as it will think it is another chameleon.

✓ Don't handle a chameleon that is behaving in a defensive or stressed manner (hissing, biting, rocking, gaping, or closing its eyes and staying motionless). You need to listen to those signals and give it space.

✓ Don't grab a chameleon by the neck, tail, back, or feet unless it is absolutely necessary.

Hunger strikes and anorexia:

The term "hunger strike" refers to a situation where a chameleon refuses to eat anything for a short period. In this case, a short period means a few days but less than a week.

The possible causes for this behavior include boredom with a limited diet, shedding, or in females who are about to lay eggs. If the cause is boredom you can add variety to your chameleon's diet. In the other two situations the animal will begin to eat again when it is ready. Regardless of the cause, a panther chameleon will not be adversely affected by such a short period without food, so there is no need to be concerned.

Anorexia, on the other hand, refers to a situation where the chameleon refuses to eat for a more extended period. This is also accompanied by other worrying symptoms such as weakness, weight loss, pallor, and lethargy. Anorexia is usually a symptom of a more serious health problem rather than a condition in and of itself.

You must take your panther chameleon to a vet so that he or she can do tests and treat the underlying problem. Some of the potential causes include nutritional imbalances; bacterial diseases; parasites; chronic stress; injuries to the mouth, tongue, or jaw; or even organ failure.

4) The risk to you of Salmonella infection

Contrary to popular belief you can't only become infected with Salmonella, a very nasty bacteria, by eating food contaminated with it. You can also get it from handling reptiles and amphibians and from their cages and the surfaces that they have been in contact with. What is especially difficult is that reptiles can carry the bacteria and look healthy.

The good news is that you can protect yourself and others in your home from Salmonella infection through good, thorough, and regular hygiene practices:

- After you have handled your panther chameleon, the items in its cage, or cleaned its cage, you must wash your hands very thoroughly with soap and warm water. Adults should supervise the washing of children's hands to make sure that it is done properly.

- Don't ever allow children under the age of five or children or adults with weak or damaged immune systems to handle your chameleon, as they will be more likely to become infected than adults with strong immune systems.

- Clean your chameleon's cage outdoors if possible.

- When you are cleaning the cage and items from it, such as branches and the pots the plants are in, you should wear disposable gloves.

- Don't pour water from a chameleon's cage into sinks or basins where food or eating/drinking utensils are washed, where people get drinking water, or into the bathtub.

- Don't touch your mouth while handling your chameleon, after you have done so, or while and after cleaning its cage.

- Wash the clothes you were wearing when you cleaned out the cage as soon as possible so bacteria isn't on the fabric. Do the same if you've handled your panther chameleon and your garments came into contact with items that could be contaminated or with your chameleon itself.

- Thoroughly wash, with a disinfectant, any surface that your chameleon has been on.

- Don't allow your panther chameleon to roam around in areas where food and drink are stored, prepared, or eaten.

Chapter 11: Breeding Them

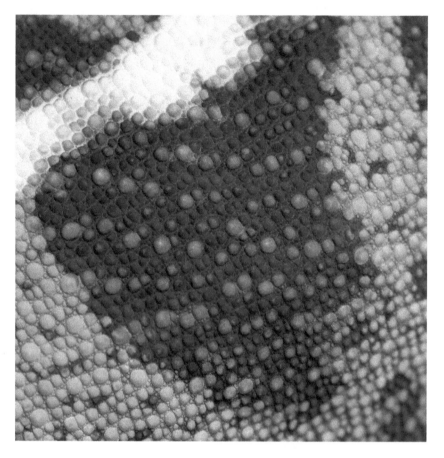

Before you can responsibly start to breed panther chameleons there are things you need to know so that you are prepared for the work that is involved and the joys and difficulties of the process.

1) Sexual maturity

Males:

Male panther chameleons reach sexual maturity when they are about six months old. This will be accompanied by behavioral and physical changes.

They become more territorial and, in the presence of rival males, they will give what are known as color displays. Usually color displays with rivals involve much darker, deeper colors. Their full, adult colors will not appear until they are about a year old, however. They will also begin to court females. This process involves softer, more muted color displays and a courtship dance that involves head bobbing.

The primary physical change once a male chameleon reaches physical maturity is that the hemipenal bulge becomes more evident because the sexual organs have reached maturity.

Females:

Females also mature at about six months. However, one should wait to do any breeding until a female is full size (when she is about a year old). The reason for this is that a full size or adult chameleon is much better able to deal with the extra calcium demands placed on her body when she produces eggs.

Female panther chameleons lay, on average, three clutches of eggs a year. There are considerable variations, though. Some individuals may only lay one clutch and others as many as five in a single year. The average number of eggs per clutch is around 25, but a clutch may contain anything from 14 to in excess of 40 eggs. The gestation period of the eggs within the female's body is also variable, but is usually three to six weeks.

2) Breeding: general information

In the wild, panther chameleons breed during the months of spring and summer. In the artificially constant climate of a cage, chameleons will breed all year round.

Both males and females adopt specific courtship colors and behaviors. They often become more intense in color in order to attract a mate and the males, when they have located a suitable and receptive female, will bob their heads up and down.

The basic color of a mature female panther chameleon when she is on her own is brown, tan, gray, or a faint green. The patterning consists of indistinct vertical bars and a lateral stripe. This is known as metachromatic. Your female panther chameleon will tell you when she is receptive to a mate so you need to watch her. When her colors and patterns change, you will know she is ready to mate. When the females become receptive their colors become a pale, but sometimes rich, pink or orange hue, and any darker bars or band she usually has become lighter and disappear. An even clearer indication is if these changes take place when she is in the presence of a male.

Usually one should place the female in the male's enclosure. Receptive females will allow males to approach them from behind. Mating or **copulation** lasts from 10-30 minutes, and the pair will mate several times in this period.

The pair should be left together in the cage until they have mated a few times or until the female's colors change to indicate that she is no longer receptive, whichever happens first. She may also indicate that she is no longer interested by hissing or rocking. You should then remove her gently and place her back in her own cage. If you leave her with the male and he continues to approach her she may become very stressed or aggressive.

If a female has become pregnant, or gravid, she will assume a distinctive color and pattern. This often consists of black with bands of pink or pale orange. In addition to this "Stay away" color, if males approach she will warn them off with threat displays such as rocking, gaping (opening her mouth very wide), and hissing.

At the end of the brief gestation period of two to three weeks, the female will dig a burrow or tunnel in which to lay her eggs. Once they are laid, she will cover the eggs with soil. Depending on conditions, the hatchlings will emerge from the soil between six and twelve months later.

You need to keep in mind that females will lay eggs even if there has not been a mate or mating. If the eggs your chameleon lays are yellow in color, then it's likely they are infertile and there won't be any hatchlings.

Finally, a female panther chameleon should not be bred more than once a year in order to keep her healthy. Female chameleons have been known to retain sperm and go on to lay two or even three clutches of eggs after a single mating.

3) Your pregnant chameleon

A gravid, or egg-carrying, female will gain a marked amount of weight even if she is not eating more than usual. Her body will look rounder. Behavior changes include restlessness and, just before laying her eggs, she may stop eating all together. A female that is about to lay eggs will start to explore the bottom of the cage looking for a good place to bury her eggs.

That is where you need to step in. In fact, you need to get ready before she is! You must provide a laying bin if you have a female panther chameleon. You should keep one in the cage on a permanent basis just in case you miss the signs that she is ready to lay or she has a laying cycling that results in her laying eggs more often than the average number of times in a year.

A laying bin is not a complex or expensive item at all. It needs to be a tray or container that is a minimum of 12 inches or 30.5 centimeters deep and 9 inches or 23 centimeters wide. This gives the female enough space and depth to dig a tunnel in which to lay her clutch of eggs.

You must fill the laying tray with fine, moistened sand or organic soil. This sand or soil must be moist enough to hold a tunnel, but neither too wet nor too dry, as this will make it impossible to create a tunnel that won't keep collapsing. When she is ready, the female will dig a tunnel to the depth that the container or laying bin allows.

A female often starts by digging test tunnels. Once she has established that the soil is the right consistency, and she is ready, she will dig the tunnel, lay her eggs in it, and then cover her tracks on the surface so that it doesn't look as though there is a tunnel there at all. She achieves this by scuffing the soil in a large area around where the tunnel mouth had been.

The entire digging, tunneling, laying, and covering process will take several hours. In some cases, it can even take a few days. Regardless of how long it takes, laying eggs leaves a female panther chameleon tired and thin, and she will need to rest and to be built up again with food that has been correctly gut loaded.

Conversely, if a female panther chameleon doesn't start digging a tunnel the first day she explores the laying bin or has access to it, don't worry; maybe she isn't ready yet. You can just try again the next day. Some females are shy and will only start to dig and lay eggs if their cage is covered so that they have privacy.

It's really important not to move your panther chameleon a lot at this stage. Don't try to handle her, and don't check on her too often. If she becomes stressed, she may become egg bound and this can pose health risks to her.

4) Special care for female or gravid chameleons

The most difficult part of owning a female panther chameleon is the laying of eggs. From the age of about six months females are able to lay eggs regardless of whether they have been in contact with a male. A chameleon will lay a clutch of eggs every few months for her entire life.

This aspect of owning female chameleons puts a lot of owners off. However, if a female is provided with a suitable laying box, a lot of these issues will be avoided.

Most female chameleons that die are lost because of becoming egg-bound or egg-binding. With this condition the eggs fuse together inside the female and can't be laid or passed through her body. This usually happens if a female has no suitable place to lay eggs and so she holds them in her body. Over time, the eggs become larger than normal and begin to stick together. Eventually the eggs form a life-threatening mass in the female's body.

If the cages of female panther chameleons are kept at a slightly cooler temperature than that of males, their metabolisms will slow down. If this happens they will often lay less often and lay far fewer eggs each time than the normal clutch average. This will extend a female's life expectancy and make her owner's life easier.

While it is true that in the majority of cases if a female lays one clutch of eggs she will go on laying the rest of her life, there is the odd individual chameleon that may only produce one or two clutches during her entire lifetime. It is not clear why this happens. Some females will also produce far fewer eggs than the species average. The trick is not to get too concerned if your panther chameleon is not text-book typical. If you are worried,

85

though, speak to the breeder you bought your pet from or consult your vet.

5) Feeding & caring for babies

Hatching:

Baby chameleons usually break through the egg and their nose becomes visible. What can be alarming is that they then lie there, motionless, for hours. In fact some don't move for days after breaking the egg. Don't assume the worst and intervene because trying to pull or cut them out can cause injury and infection. What they are probably doing is resting after the demands of breaking the shell, feeding on the remaining egg yolk in the shell, and getting ready to come out and face the world.

The first few days:

An odd phenomenon is that once one hatchling has been brave enough to emerge, the others all follow.

You can certainly feed your new baby chameleons, but it is not unusual for them not to eat for a day or two. Keep in mind that they ate before hatching…

Housing babies:

Some panther chameleon owners and breeders use cages called butterfly cages for hatchlings. They are great for babies because they are made from a fine, soft mesh that is unlikely to injure the hatchlings and because they open and close by means of a zipper. A good-sized cage for babies is approximately 24"L x 12"W x 24"H.

Crucial aspects to keep in mind are that babies also need plants, even if it's only one or two small ones in their cage. Hatchlings and babies are also extremely sensitive to changes in the temperature in their cages. You therefore have to monitor it very closely. High temperatures are especially dangerous as very young chameleons become dehydrated even faster than adult panther chameleons do.

Babies don't need a basking bulb, but a UV bulb is necessary so that they can produce the vitamin D3 they need. The general temperature should be round about 70 degrees Fahrenheit or 21 degrees Centigrade. Bulbs should be suspended above the cage and not placed in it so that the babies don't overheat or burn themselves.

Finally, if you have large groups of babies, you need to divide them into groups of 10 or even fewer. This prevents the smaller ones from being bullied or attacked by the larger and stronger ones and not having a chance to eat. Stress can be a killer with baby chameleons too and often much faster than it is with adults.

Feeding and watering babies:

Once the babies show interest in food, they need to be given food two or three times a day. As with adults, baby chameleons need variety in their diet. Some breeders suggest a combination of small feeder insects: fruit flies, ants, pinhead crickets, and roach nymphs, for example.

The food can get bigger as the babies grow and are able to catch and swallow larger insects. With pre-adults you can dust the food with a little calcium, but they are still too young for any of the supplements that are given to adult or fully grown panther chameleons. They also need daily exposure to natural sunlight and a UV bulb so they can manufacture the vitamin D3 they need for healthy bone development.

When you water or spray take care not to spray the hatchlings or babies directly. You need to make sure, though, that—as with the adults—the leaves of their plants are wet so they have enough to drink.

The fecal matter of a baby panther chameleon should be white in color. If it's orange it means that the babies are suffering from dehydration, and you need to address this immediately or they will die!

Chapter 12: Prices, Costs, and Where to Buy Them

1) Costs

The cost to purchase a panther chameleon:

These amazing lizards do not come cheap! A panther chameleon will set you back between $140 and $600. That is just for the chameleon itself. On top of that you will need to pay for all the equipment you will need before you can even take your new pet home.

Set-up costs:

You need certain basic equipment for your chameleon. These once-off costs include:

- *Cage*: ranges from $30 to $300.

- *Lighting*:

    - UV bulb: from $20 to $70.

    - Heat bulb (40 or 60w) for basking area: $2 to $6.

    - Light fixtures: $10 for a linear UV fixture and $5 for the heat bulb fixture.

- *Supplements*: An all-in-one product will cost $9. A Phosphorous-free calcium product and multivitamins will cost between $6 and $12.

- *Watering system*: The costs will depend of the level of sophistication of the system you choose:

- A spray bottle or pump sprayer costs between $1 and $20.

- Drip system: $15. If you buy the items you need and make it yourself, it will cost less.

- Automatic misting system: these systems range in price from about $100 to about $200.

- *Plants*: The best plants are live ones, and you should buy enough to give your panther chameleon cover and hunting pathways. Because the size of the cage and the number of plants each owner buys vary, it is difficult to provide a cost estimate, but an average of $55 should probably be budgeted for. Branches are easy enough to find for most chameleon owners, but you need to ensure they are clean.

So, buying a pet chameleon will cost you at least $300 on set-up costs, excluding the price of the chameleon itself. You may be able to buy items, including second-hand or pre-owned ones, more cheaply online, but then you need to think about how clean these items might be.

If you do buy used cages, etc. online you will need to disinfect all items thoroughly or you run the risk of infecting your new panther chameleon with bacteria or parasites. What you save on second hand items you might have to spend later on vet bills, so weigh the pros and cons carefully!

Average monthly costs:

These expenses include all the items you need for regular, routine maintenance and hygiene and for the overall health and well-being of your pet lizard. They obviously don't include any emergencies or unforeseen extras that you may encounter such as vet bills, for example.

- o *Food*: This will vary depending on how much you buy at a time. Buying in bulk can save you money, but you need to be able to house and feed the insects you purchase.

    - Insects: $20 to $60 depending on type and quantity.

    - Insect housing: $5 to $12 depending on size and type.

- o *Lights*:

    - UV bulb: from $20 to $70.

    - Heat bulb: $2 to $6 for a standard household 40 or 60 watt bulb.

- o *Supplements*:

    - An all-in-one product: $9.

    - Phosphorous-free calcium product and multivitamins: $6 to $12 for a container.

- o *Gut loading food*: This must consist of a mixture of dry gut load and fresh fruits and vegetables. The combination you buy, how many insects and chameleons you have to feed, and the amount you need to get as a result, will obviously affect the cost.

Medical or emergency costs:

It is impossible to give an estimate of how much these will be and how often you will have to incur them. Your chameleon may stay healthy. On the flip side, panther chameleons do get sick sometimes.

Some owners suggest that it's a good idea to have between $100 and $200 saved or set aside in case your chameleon suddenly needs medical attention.

You should also ask your vet to check for parasites by doing a fecal test twice a year. These kinds of tests will cost in the region of $15 to $20 each.

The option to purchase pet insurance:

If you give your panther chameleon the right diet and supplements, the correct environment, enough water, and perform all the necessary cleaning and maintenance, it should stay healthy. Of course, no animal is completely safe from illness, and even the healthiest lizard can be injured. In addition, vet care is becoming more expensive.

Enter pet insurance. Depending on where you are you may be able to opt to take out one of several types of coverage to help you with bills when your panther chameleon needs medical care. Some insurers offer the choice of a plan that covers expenses in the event of an accident only. Others will pay costs for both accident and illness. The third option, one that usually gets added onto one of the others, is to cover routine items like parasite tests.

Like most insurance, these policies will have a deductible or excess that you will have to pay, but they can help greatly if your chameleon ever requires significant or ongoing treatment or vet care. The premium and affordability will also vary depending on

93

the type of coverage chosen and how many chameleons you place on the policy.

Your vet should be able to supply you with a brochure or information. An Internet search should also find various suppliers of pet insurance that you can contact for more information and their rates.

You will have to decide whether to take out a policy by weighing the cost of insurance against the possibility of being out of pocket at a later date.

2) Where you can buy a Panther Chameleon

United States of America:

➤ *Screameleons* (screameleons.com): Screameleons is based in Virginia in the USA although they supply chameleons and items related to their care across the States. They sell a wide range of panther chameleons and offer an "arrive alive" and health guarantee. In addition, they sell equipment for chameleon owners, including kits for owners of various experience levels, and they offer an online helpline to their customers.

➤ *FLChams* (flchams.com): FL Chams sells a number of types of chameleons including the panther chameleon. They also sell a range of cages, owner's kits, books on chameleons and their care, and other equipment a chameleon owner may need.

➤ *Backwater Reptiles* (backwaterreptiles.com): In addition to selling a range of panther chameleons they claim that they breed themselves, this company sells feeder insects, cages, other equipment, and they offer free shipping on the items bought from them. There are also care sheets available via their website.

➢ *Kammerflage Kreations* (chameleonsonly.com): They specialize in selling panther chameleons, but they do also offer a few other chameleon species. Their website provides very helpful practical advice for chameleon owners, and their online store offers all of the items one would need to set up or maintain a cage in addition to books, gift certificates, gut loads, and even novelty chameleon-related items such as ornaments and key chains.

United Kingdom:

➢ *Chameleoco* (chameleoco.co.uk): They sell a very wide range of reptiles including panther chameleons. Their website contains a number of helpful articles for both newcomers and more experienced chameleon owners. The online store offers all of the items one would need to set up or maintain a cage.

➢ *Exotic Pets* (exotic-pets.co.uk): This company sells a range of panther chameleons, and they also offer clients feeder insects, cages, and equipment. Their website also offers numerous articles and fact or care sheets and details of events of interest to chameleon owners.

➢ *Blue Lizard Retiles* (bluelizardreptiles.co.uk): This site offers a very wide range of reptiles, including panther chameleons, for sale. They also offer cages, equipment, etc. through their online store.

Conclusion

Dos... in no particular order

- ✓ Ensure the cage is large enough for an adult chameleon.

- ✓ Provide a laying bin for females.

- ✓ Monitor your chameleon's health so you spot problems early on.

- ✓ Mist your panther chameleon's cage at least twice a day to prevent dehydration.

- ✓ Ensure that the temperature and humidity levels are where they should be at all times.

✓ Keep your chameleon's cage in a quiet, low traffic area.

✓ Feed it suitable types and sizes of food.

✓ Feed it a variety of foods.

✓ Provide plenty of plants and vines for exploring, climbing, and hunting.

✓ Include a basking spot in the cage.

✓ Take your panther chameleon outside for doses of natural sunlight.

✓ Invest in real plants and get branches.

✓ Set up a regular schedule in terms of misting, feeding, and lighting.

✓ Have parasite tests done regularly by the vet.

✓ Keep the cage really clean at all times.

Don'ts... in no particular order

- Don't handle your panther chameleon too often.

- Don't be impatient when you do take it out of the cage and handle it.

- Don't move fast around your chameleon.

- Don't leave your chameleon in the sun for too long or without shade to move into.

- Don't place bowls of water or fountains in the cage.

- Don't place lights and bulbs in the cage where your panther chameleon can get burned by them.

And in closing...

You really need to take being a panther chameleon owner seriously. This commitment must begin before you even bring your new pet home.

It is estimated that in America between 50-90% of all reptile pets die during their first year in captivity. Even if only a small percentage of these reptiles consist of panther chameleons, that is an appalling number! It's also a statistic you don't want your chameleon to be part of.

This guide's primary purpose is to make sure that you have the information that you need to decide, first and foremost, if this is really the right pet for you, your spouse, or your child.

If the answer is a confident and honest *Yes!*, then this pet owner's guide will also give you the details that will help you to keep your panther chameleon healthy and happy.

All animals in captivity should at least live to their usual or expected life span. In fact, given they are safe from their natural predators and receive a good diet and vet care, they should exceed the average life span for their species. However, this is often not the case with reptiles including chameleons because owners:

❖ Don't understand what is involved in caring properly for a panther chameleon

❖ Get really bad information and advice from less than scrupulous dealers or importers who just want to make a sale and so avoid talking about the challenges of owning and caring for a chameleon

❖ Provide an unsuitable cage and living environment

❖ Can't afford the regular maintenance and feeding costs

❖ Can't afford to pay for medical care when it is necessary

❖ Just plain get bored because they can't play with it, take it for walks, etc.

❖ Find that caring for a chameleon is too much like work and get lazy

On a more upbeat note, if you are one of those individuals who commits to owning and caring for one of these amazing lizards, you will be rewarded by having a pet that is fascinating, beautiful, and fulfilling. Enjoy your panther chameleon and teach others about these wonderful reptiles!

If you read information on chameleon care online, in books, or in magazines, you will see that there are various, sometimes conflicting, views and ideas about how to best house and care for a panther chameleon, the best types of lighting to use in the cage, how to go about feeding, what to do about supplements, and how to breed these fabulous reptiles. Your own experiences may also provide you with information and ideas that differ from those you read.

Remember… there is no definitive, single "right" way to care for a panther chameleon. As you get to know your pet you will learn more and more and refine your care of your specific pet.